THE MISSING LEADER

One Man's Journey to Leading Well

A Leadership Fable

MICHAEL HOLLAND

Bishop House
CONSULTING

ISBN 978-0-9848893-7-2

Thank you to Barbara, my beautiful wife and partner in life.

CONTENTS

THE NOTE

Jacob stood frozen next to the bed in his hotel room. He picked up the small piece of paper that had fallen from his suitcase into that small space between the bed and the wall. He almost missed seeing it fall. He opened the note and immediately recognized the handwriting.

Jacob – I Miss You

Jacob went to bed that night but didn't sleep well, tossing and turning, thinking about work and that note he found. What did the note mean?

THE SPEECH

Jacob pushed his way between two others to grab a coffee mug. He had just a few minutes at the breakfast buffet to get a hot coffee and a bagel before going into the small ballroom at the hotel. His phone buzzed in his pocket. Probably his boss following up with some emails from their 6:30 am conference call. Jacob ignored the buzzing, gathered his food and hurried to find a seat.

He arrived just in time for the final moments of the introduction for the speaker. Jacob wasn't sure this conference was the best use of his time, but his friend Chuck highly recommended it to him.

The cordial applause died down as the speaker bounded onto the stage. "Hi, I'm David and I'm a leader in a little company where we've learned the true meaning of what it takes to lead well.

"I'm here today to tell you about a transformation that has been occurring in our little corner of the world. About five years ago some colleagues and I set ourselves upon a quest to awaken the sleeping leadership giants within the youngest of our leaders.

"We believed that too many young leaders were following in the misplaced footsteps of the leaders who walked before them. Upon promotion, these young leaders increased their time at work, staying later and then working remotely from home late at night. They began attending meetings for six, seven or eight hours a day. They barked out orders to their former teammates and struggled with understanding the real role of a leader.

"Our young leaders were leaving families and communities in their wake. While they went to the house they called home, they were more like zombies than parents and spouses. They carried

4

the baggage of work on their shoulders, dumping the stress and negative energy upon their kids and spouse. Basically, they were just attending another meeting that just happened to be at a different location with different people.

"They stood on the sidelines at their kids' soccer games – at least at those games they attended – eyes glued to the small screen on their smart phones. These young leaders looked up at the game when the rush of the crowd signaled something big was happening. Only they missed the pass young junior made to the player who ultimately passed the ball to the goal scorer. They missed the little pass that was so important.

"These young leaders didn't lead badly, at least by typical standards to which we hold leaders, but they left so much opportunity on the table. They didn't realize the full value of their role in enabling an environment that allows employees to excel and love being at work. They seldom understood their personal leadership style and the impact their communications were having on all those around them. They undervalued the time and energy investment required to build trusted relationships with employees and peers and bosses. They called the small group a 'team' without any inclination that the group felt nothing like a team.

"Today, five years later, we now have young leaders who are fully engaged at work and at home and in our community. We have healthy leaders who grasp the gravity of their responsibility to not only build stable environments for employees to excel at work, but also to build stable environments at home for kids and spouses to excel at life.

"We now have cohesive teams producing at levels four or five times as high as before, while working less total hours. Yes, you heard that correctly. . . teams are four to five times more productive than before, WHILE working less total hours.

"Employees go home to families that are more

functional. Parents who arrive home free of the burden of emotional work baggage with a little jump in their step. They are more patient with their kids and spouse, creating windows of opportunity for small conversations about nothing. Yes, you heard that right as well, conversations about nothing.

"Our community now has fully engaged parents attending soccer games and even volunteering to coach, bringing their highly leverageable team-building skills to these young members of our community."

Jacob listened. He shook his head in slight defiance. He felt the pit of his stomach ache. Then he thought about the note. What did Abby mean that she missed him? Was that just a sweet note from his loving wife? Or a desperate hand reaching out for help . . . or to help?

Jacob did a quick review and analysis of the last six months of his marriage.

- How many nights had he missed dinner with the family?
- How often was he on his laptop after the kids went to bed?
- On their vacation, did he really work every morning from 4:30 am to 7:30 am before the family woke up?
- When was his last date night with Abby?

Jacob wasn't happy with the analysis. But what could he do? He had to work the hours he worked in order to be successful in his role and have the opportunity to be promoted.

This speaker was full of it; there's no way that all those leaders were able to extract that high level of productivity from their employees while working less hours. No way.

And what's all this noise about relationships with employees. His team trusted him and he had good relationships across the board.

WALKING WITH A WISE MAN

Jacob hustled through the lobby of the hotel and as his phone buzzed he began the juggle of all he was holding to get to his phone. The coffee began to spill as Jacob awkwardly leaned sideways, attempting to keep everything in its place.

"Hey, let me grab that coffee for you."

It was David, the speaker, who was also hustling through the lobby. Jacob handed David the coffee, answered his phone and talked in spurts with his boss. David stood patiently, holding Jacob's coffee a couple of yards away, giving him personal space for his call.

Jacob finished his call and thanked David for his help.

"Everything all right there, sport?"

"Yeah, I'm just trying to keep everything moving forward while I'm at this conference. My friend Chuck suggested I come but it's so tough being away and remotely managing my team and keeping up with my boss' questions."

"Hey, I have a question for you David."

"Great, I love questions. What's on your mind?"

"You mentioned that the teams those young leaders were leading became more productive, in fact extremely more productive, while working less hours. That sure sounds like an exaggeration."

"So, what's your question?"

"Okay, assuming your claims about productivity are true, what changed? I mean, specifically, what did those leaders do to get their teams to be that much more productive?"

"Well, the short answer is they learned to lead well as true leaders, deeply understanding their role as a leader. Would you like to hear the long answer to your question?"

"Uh, yeah, I would, I think" said Jacob glancing at the clock "but the next session starts in 30 minutes and I have a ton of email to triage before then as well as a couple of calls to make."

"Your call, sport. I'm more than willing to invest the next 30 minutes with you and I think you'll be very intrigued with the long answer. Most aspiring leaders are very curious about what it takes to be a leader who leads well."

Jacob stared at David. He hadn't heard someone speak in this way before. Leading well? What does that mean? He thinks I'm an aspiring leader and not already a leader? But I am curious; there must be something logical that moved the needle on the productivity.

"Okay, I'm in. Let's grab a seat over there."

For the next 30 minutes David provided Jacob with the background on the role of the leader.

"To lead well, it's critical for leaders at all levels, and particularly young leaders, to grasp the real role of a leader. So often our best professionals are thrown into a position of a leader because they were the best among their peers on the team. They are moved up to manage their former peers and most often receive no training regarding what the role of a leader demands.

"So, we started our young leaders at square one and used a rather simple model to depict the critical role of a leader."

David continued "Think of a wheel from a bike. You have the hub in the middle supporting a bunch of spokes, which extend from there to connect the rim and tire to the hub. The sturdiness of the hub is critically important to the whole wheel. The spokes are delicately connected to the hub and with many spokes, the rim and tire are held in place. A strong hub anchoring the spokes can allow for a wheel to roll true and straight, while carrying a heavy load."

"You with me so far?"

"Yeah, I'm with you" Jacob answered.

"The hub is your personal leadership style. Developing deep awareness of your leadership style enables you to know how best to maximize the style to influence and guide others as the situation dictates.

"The spokes represent employees. Self-aware, mature leaders leverage their understanding of their personal leadership style to cultivate and embrace employees with a single goal: to build trusted relationships. You want strong connections between your spokes and the hub; likewise, you want strong relationships between the leader and his employees.

"The spokes culminate in their connection to the rim which represents teams. Through trusted relationships, mature leaders motivate and inspire employees to form cohesive teams. And cohesive teams outperform all other teams hands down because they have the strength of all those employees working together for a common goal or purpose.

"So, to summarize,

- The Hub – your personal leadership style
- The Spokes – your employees
- The Rim – your cohesive team

Make sense?"

WHY THE HUB IS SO CRITICAL

David saw that Jacob was engaged but still looked a bit weary. "The primary opportunity that young leaders miss is learning about their own personal leadership styles early in their careers as leaders. Leaders need to first understand themselves and be fully in tune with how they communicate and lead. The clarity of communication comes with gaining knowledge of your preferred communication style and that of others. We used a wonderful toolset – the *Everything DiSC Workplace®* and *Everything DiSC® Management* assessments – to provide leaders with the knowledge they needed to understand their natural or preferred styles and the personal dynamics that take place among varying styles.

"DiSC", "Everything DiSC" and "Everything DiSC Workplace" are registered trademarks of John Wiley & Sons, Inc.

"As leaders we know that while we easily communicate with some employees, others are very difficult for us. Understanding the underlying personality styles is difficult. Seeking to understand how people of certain styles like to communicate and often behave is hard as well. But doing so provides a leader with intimate knowledge of and intelligence about how someone is likely to be motivated, act under stress, behave when excited and interact in social engagements.

"A key leadership competency for leaders at all levels is being able to turn the dials of their own leadership behaviors up and/or down in order to enable influential outcomes in others. In other words, to guide those with whom they work.

"Leaders who deeply explore their leadership style gain a deep awareness of **why** they lead.

"Have you ever thought about that question? Why do you lead others?"

Jacob thought and then answered "I would think compensation is an important reason."

"Yes." replied David. "The most often cited and simplest answer is because of the pay and entitlements. But there must be a deeper reason why. And the exploration of this why enables leaders to develop keen awareness to the purpose for **their** work as a leader.

"Leaders start in the same place: wanting to help those around them. Pretty simple. But why do they want to help others?

"When leaders invest the time and energy to really understand their personal leadership style, they awaken to seeing opportunities where they could be more effective. They begin to realize that there is more capacity available within themselves to leverage. The other way to look at these opportunities is as gaps in one's leadership capacity which can be closed or bridged. But we have to choose to bridge the gap and create habits to leverage the opportunities. So one of these opportunities is enabling relationship margin.

"Superficial relationships with employees are easy but there is little relationship margin available."

"David, hold on a second. What is relationship margin?"

"Relationship margin can be defined as the space, latitude, energy and time offered to you from a trusted relationship. Understanding both how you react to and how others perceive your reaction to pressure, delegation, conflict, stress, and success creates relationship margin. This margin is a delay in reaction from someone with whom you are interacting.

"Let's take a real life example. You mentioned that your friend Chuck told you about this conference. How do you know Chuck?"

"Chuck and I went to college together and

worked for several years afterwards at the same small company. He's one of my really close friends." Jacob answered.

"Great. So if Chuck came into your office one day visibly upset, really mad about something and started to let loose with a barrage of curse words, would you begin yelling back at him?"

"No, of course not. He's upset about something but not at me." Jacob responded.

"Right!" exclaimed David. "You know him, trust him and because of your relationship, you give him that understanding and that's what we call relationship margin.

"As a mature, self-actualized leader, you can invest in building more trusted relationships with your employees and they will in turn give you the benefit of the doubt when they start to sense your reaction to a situation. They'll hesitate in reacting because they know you and trust you. While that hesitation may be just a split second or several seconds, it creates the space of time generating a window of opportunity for you to read the situation and appropriately adjust your style and interaction.

"A second gap or opportunity is creating and sustaining momentum. You first must fully understand how and why your personal momentum fluctuates. Then, seek to understand how you de-motivate others in certain situations, both intentionally and unintentionally. Your goal is to reach a level of self-actualization wherein you understand how you can increase your motivation behaviors while decreasing your demotivation behaviors both directly and through the leaders who may work for you.

"The overarching goal is to build your leadership maturity which grows primarily through gaining wisdom from as many experiences and interactions as possible. Mature leaders gather intelligence from all interactions – even boring meetings – to add to their understanding of human dynamics. They watch and listen. And then they think about what they have seen and heard.

"Mature leaders also have high emotional intelligence: they are socially aware enough to self-manage themselves so that they can build strong relationships. Emotional intelligence can be built over time and a key building component is seeking to understand how you have impacted the dynamics of situations and interactions both in good ways and in ways that could be improved.

"Our catchy little phrase on this theme was 'Immature leaders act. Mature leaders think, act, and reflect.'

"When you have a group of leaders in an organization who collectively increase their leadership maturity, the organization gains leadership capacity which is a tremendous asset."

THAT NOTE

Jacob was intrigued. He might not fully grasp how this leadership model was going to change the world but he did feel like he had a better understanding of his role.

"There's my phone buzzing again." Jacob reached into his pocket to pull out the phone but instead pulled out a piece of paper. The note. He had forgotten all about the note. As he stared at the writing he sighed deeply. David leaned over and asked, "So what's the story behind that note?"

Jacob wasn't sure how to answer the question to his new friend, though he felt extremely and uncharacteristically comfortable. He handed the note to David and described his lost state of understanding.

David waited. He let the awkward silence hang in the air, allowing Jacob the opportunity to find the words he wanted to speak.

Jacob told David the story of the note falling from his suitcase and barely seeing it drop between the bed and the wall. Jacob described the tension at home with Abby and their two active kids. How he was so much busier at work with the new leadership role, how he had to be successful, how he was missing more and more dinners at home or just barely arriving in time to sit down at dinner. How when he tried to engage in conversations at home, it felt eerily similar to his role at work, putting out fires and solving problems.

"Thank you for sharing more about your story Jacob." David said kindly. "That's amazing that Abby had the courage to write that note to you. So many of us allow others to drive our lives in ways that we don't intend or desire.

"While I don't recall any 'Abbys' who had the

courage to write the note you received last night, I have seen far too many couples whose families were torn apart in divorce because of the words on that note. I guess that's part of the reason my colleagues and I were so invested in changing the next generation of leaders. We were sick and tired of watching so many families crumble under the weight of the work our companies were putting on the shoulders of ill-prepared and inexperienced leaders. We hadn't done anything different than had been done with us and that was the problem. We knew first-hand about the impacts but were afraid to make waves.

"That all ended when we decided it was our responsibility not just to lead but to lead **well**.

"That our jobs were not about the pay and entitlements but about building the community of employees and cultures which would drive healthy behaviors."

THE MISSING LEADER

PARENTING STYLE

"What was the change?" asked Jacob. "What was the catalyst?"

"Well," David said, "the main catalyst was a small talk a friend of mine gave me as I struggled with a situation not much different than yours. My friend listened to my complaints and then looked me squarely in the eye and said he had tone, was locked in and asked if he had permission to fire."

"Permission to fire?"

"Yes, you know, the movie Top Gun? Tom Cruise is in the middle of a dog fight with his fighter jet. He gets the enemy fighter jet in his sights, radar locks in, the crosshairs align, and while the screen changes color to a deep red, a loud tone can be heard followed by the pilot almost yelling 'I've got tone. . . I'm going to take the shot. . . Firing'

"So I said, yea, of course I'm ready. So he told me that truth was my friend and the truth as he saw it was that I had this great leadership model I was deploying at work with my colleagues and we were starting to see some success. But we were missing the other half of the population: our families. We should be taking our wheel thingy and looking at how we deploy at home.

"And there it was. We needed to overlay our model onto our families.

- The Hub – my parenting style
- The Spokes – my kids and spouse
- The Rim – our functional family

"As parents, we need to deeply understand our communication styles and the natural styles with which we lead our families so that we can build solid, trusted relationships with our kids and spouses in order to build functional families.

"What's unique in a family though, is that the parents need to first have a healthy, loving, vibrant marriage so that they can lead the family together each leveraging their own communications style while parenting.

"Building functional families requires work, dedication and investment of time. And it's the latter one that trips up most leaders as they try to manage the tension between home and work.

"We rationalize that the time we invest at work is for the benefit of our families to a point that we can become obsessed with moving forward and up. We spend most of our prime time during the week at work, doing work and/or thinking about work.

"In addition, we can get caught up with constantly moving the goal line regarding our finances. Imagine if you we're playing in a football league over a number of years and as you became a better, stronger athlete allowing you to run faster, you kept moving the goal line further and further away. Then you train longer and harder to get faster only to move the goal line again as you improve.

We do the same thing with our financial goals in our magical spreadsheets that document our plans for our financial futures. We create our goals for generating wealth to be prepared for life and pay for some of our kids' college and to begin preparing for retirement. Then as we get raises, we tinker with the future values of the financial goals raising the bar of what we 'need' which in turn drives us to perceive a need to work harder to get more promotions and more raises to reach the new goal.

"We challenged our leaders to answer these questions.

- What if we all used our original financial goal numbers as our current goal for financial achievement?

- How might we look differently at the world around us?

- How might we look at our goals and desires and rewards?

- How might we help others to start college or get a little help over a financial bump in the road?"

THE MISSING LEADER

SEEING A NEW WORLD

Jacob was overwhelmed. He woke up today thinking he was doing fine. He was keeping most of the balls in the air and felt like he was surviving. Now, he wasn't sure what to think. Was he blowing it at work as a leader? Was he blowing it at home as a father and husband?

David had seen this blank stare before. He knew Jacob's mind was just opened up to a whole new world and he would need some time to digest the new concepts.

"Jacob" . . . David leaned in to talk more softly to Jacob.

"As you travel home this evening I want you to use a concept of lenses to help you think through our discussion. You've been wearing a set of glasses which allowed you to see but were actually murky. You didn't realize they were murky. Now you've cleaned the glasses up a bit and the world around you looks a little different.

"If you'd like, we could get together in a couple of weeks and you could report in on where this journey may be taking you. Also, I'll have my executive coach send you an email invitation to take the *Everything DiSC Workplace®* assessment and after you've completed the assessment, he'll give you a coaching debrief on the assessment over the phone. I want to make sure you have a full grasp of how the tool works."

Jacob nodded yes somewhat hesitantly. He wasn't quite sure what "report in" meant, nor was he sure he really wanted to keep thinking about these concepts. But he did know that he wasn't content to be just another statistic. He wanted to be a very good leader and father and husband. And he was curious about his communications style.

THE RIDE HOME

Jacob's drive home was difficult. Intellectually he was intrigued with all that David had said. But could he really adjust his behaviors successfully?

Jacob thought about the assessment David wanted him to take. What kind of test would that be and what might be revealed?

He wondered what his employees would think of him as he tried new behaviors. Wouldn't they think he was crazy? That he had gone off to this seminar and now was just trying out some new-fangled management approach that surely wouldn't last more than a week. And what about his boss, how would he react to his changes?

Jacob, as he often did, talked with God while he

drove. He asked God to help him know what to do with the wisdom David had imparted and to give him the perseverance he'd need to make changes in his approach to leadership and life.

Before he knew it, it was 10:30 pm and he was pulling into his driveway. His phone rang. He looked down and it was his boss. He decided he had to answer this call since he had been ignoring all of his calls and text messages for the last several hours.

Jacob stayed in the car for 15 minutes talking with his boss and then started walking towards his front door. As he opened the front door, he was closing out the conversation when he accidently hung up on his boss just as he stepped into the house.

ABBY

As Jacob came through the door, Abby was on the couch waiting up for him to come home. Jacob had his phone in one hand and struggled with his suitcase and backpack. Abby started to get up to greet him but when she noticed he was using his phone she sat back down and turned back to the TV she was watching.

Jacob made the connection of her movement away from him. His typical habit was to shrug off the gesture and assume Abby was being polite to allow him space for his re-entry to the house and time to finish up the work email or text. But he now saw a different path he could take. That lens was a bit clearer.

He put everything down on the floor, walked to

the family room and handed Abby the note.

Abby looked away as her eyes started to tear up. She didn't want Jacob to see how lost she really was.

Jacob walked between the couch and the coffee table, sliding onto the couch right next to Abby so that she would have to look at him. And he asked the question: "Tell me what prompted you to write this note." Their eyes met and he could see the deep anguish and pain she was feeling as she struggled to find the words to start this conversation.

"Was he really asking her to talk about this? Would he really stay for a whole conversation?" Abby thought to herself.

Just then his phone buzzed. He'd left it on the floor by the door and it was doing its own buzz dance on the hardwood floor. Abby pulled back, thinking Jacob was going to make a run for the phone. But he reached for her hand and said again,

"Please tell me what prompted you to write this note."

The next three hours were filled with deep conversations, a few too many tears and a solemn quiet that gave the sense of an end of an era.

Jacob told Abby all about his time with David and the models of leadership and parenting. How he was so confused and at ease all at the same time.

THE ASSESSMENT

The next day around noon Jacob received an email with an invitation to take the assessment David had mentioned, the *Everything DiSC® Workplace*. He started to jump to the next email but remembered David saying the assessment would only take about 15 minutes.

Jacob clicked the link and quickly became engrossed in the questions. Before he knew it, the assessment was completed. His personalized report was available immediately and he began to read through his report. He was mesmerized with the results. How could such a simple assessment be so on target.

Jacob saw that he was a "Di" style, which was described as combination of Dominance and

Influence with a general goal of being very active and pushing to reach ambitious goals. Jacob was fascinated with how the report outlined his priorities that shape his workplace experience.

Taking Action – You want things to happen quickly, so you usually hit the ground running. You may grow impatient if something slows your rapid pace, and you expect others to do what's necessary to keep up. Most likely, your sense of adventure allows you to make quick decisions without much worry about the consequences. Your willingness to take fast action can help the group make swift progress.

Getting Results – People with the Di style are ambitious and focused on success. Furthermore, you tend to set the bar high and won't settle for minor victories. You favor plans that will yield the biggest payoffs, and you're probably energized by innovation and risk. Your drive and intensity might be intimidating for others, but you're willing to do what it takes to achieve goals and get results.

Generating Enthusiasm – Like others with the Di style, you tend to maintain a high energy level, even in the face of adversity. Most likely, you're passionate about your ideas, and your outward expression allows others to see your vision as clearly as you do. Furthermore, your confidence often inspires people to jump on board. Because you believe shared excitement for a common goal is important, you place a high value on generating enthusiasm.

Jacob read the whole report and thought deeply about how he might come across to his team when he's stressed and how his style may influence how he delegates work and projects to his team.

Later that week, Jacob got together with the executive coach on the phone to debrief on his *Everything DiSC®* report. Jacob had watched an introductory video on the coach's website, providing an overview of the *Everything DiSC®* model and styles. He was amazed at just how different people can be, especially people who have a natural inclination to collaborating and inclusive interactions.

The executive coach had also had Jacob take the *Everything DiSC® Management* version of the assessment which spoke directly to how Jacob's style might be revealed during management activities such as delegating.

During the debrief, Jacob learned about the intensity of his style and talked at length about how a majority of his team likely have styles opposite of his. Jacob started to realize how different he was in his approach to work than most of his team and how he unknowingly was likely putting extra pressure on his team just by how he naturally communicates.

It was interesting to Jacob that his style in the additional assessment was exactly the same - he was still a "Di" - but two of his priorities on the DiSC® Map had changed, which better reflected management activity phrasing. Jacob was intrigued as he read through his *Everything DiSC® Management* style report regarding what priorities shape his management experience.

Taking Action – Like other managers with the Di style, you like to take command of situations and hit the ground running. You tend to move forward, while pushing your team members to keep up with your rapid pace. Most likely, you're willing to take action without much worry about the consequences, and you may become impatient with people who stand in the way of swift progress.

Displaying Drive – You often set ambitious goals, and you may encourage your team to share this focus on achievement. New ideas and adventurous options tend to energize you, and you may favor strategies that yield the biggest payoff for your efforts. You usually set the bar high and are willing to take some risks along the way. Because being driven is important to you, you tend to do what it takes to get the results you're after.

Providing Encouragement – Managers with the Di style want members of the team to feel good about their contributions and often emphasize what they're doing right when discussing their work. Because you want people to feel energized and optimistic, you probably avoid appearing overly critical. You focus on providing encouragement to give them the confidence needed to put their best foot forward.

The coach encouraged Jacob to read deeply about the other styles and particularly how he could adjust his style to better align with most of his team. Luckily, the report had tons of information for him to utilize.

AT WORK

The next several weeks at work were challenging for Jacob. He tried to put in place some of the concepts David spoke of, but old habits are so hard to break. And his head was spinning with all the information he had learned about his communication and management styles.

First, he considered how he might strengthen his relationships with his employees. Based on one of the coach's suggestions, he made a list of employees and created a schedule he would use to meet with each employee each week.

All started off well. The first meeting with each employee started off about the same with a slight awkwardness, but soon enough the employee was talking about the work he'd been doing, some of his recent successes and what he thought Jacob could do to help him be better equipped for his work.

But by the third week, Jacob was postponing these meetings as the demands for his time by others crept in as "higher" priorities. The draw to meet the demands of more powerful leaders and time sensitive projects was too much for Jacob.

Managing the tension between his time at work and home tuned out to be very difficult as well. He worked hard to find a balance that would work. For the first week he came home every day within a time window which allowed for him to interact with Abby and the kids before sitting down for dinner. The second week he made it four out of five nights. But by the third week, he was back into his old pattern, calling from work when he was supposed to already be at home.

He struggled more now because he had new insight to the damage he was causing to everyone. He started to wonder if he should ever have taken the promotion. But now he and Abby were enjoying their adjusted income. Where would his career land if he backtracked out of a management position?

REPORT-IN #1

David and Jacob met for coffee at a Panera Bread in a town which was about an hour's drive for each of them. They caught up with some small talk for a bit and then Jacob decided it was time to move the conversation forward.

"So, David, you used some wording when we were last together that I don't quite understand. You said we would get together so I could 'report in.' What exactly does that mean?"

"Sorry about that. Guess I was slipping into my comfort zone. Reporting in is the phrasing we adopted to prompt an open-ended conversation to allow young leaders to tell us what's been going on. We took the phrasing from the military schema wherein you've been out in the field for a while and now are back in base camp and ready to debrief on what you've seen, experienced, felt while out in the field leading your team.

"You're the one out there leading. You need to bring me up to speed with whatever you deem important to give me a good sense of what you've been up against, where you've succeeded, where you've stumbled and what you've learned along the way.

"So, what have you been up to?"

Jacob thought for a moment. He understood the metaphor, but it was strange that David just wanted him to start talking, almost randomly, about what he's been doing with his team.

Questions flooded his brain: where do I start? How deep do I go? Will he think I'm stupid talking about some of the petty people issues that took up so much of my time. Should I tell him about Abby? No, can't go there. Ok, I'll just give him some highlights.

Jacob spent the next ten minutes giving David a series of headlines and minimal detail on all the issues he's been dealing with since they last met. David listened and then asked some questions.

"So, tell me about your team. How would you rate the engagement of your employees with you? Do they trust you? Do they trust each other?"

Huh? What on earth was David talking about? Why is he using that trust word for my employees? Of course they trust me and each other.

"What do you mean, David, regarding trust? Of course my employees trust me and each other. We're all honest people and work hard."

"Well, one of the key mistakes young leaders make is undervaluing the significance that trust plays in building solid relationships. Trust is one of those words we've all thrown around so much that it loses it's real meaning.

"Building and embracing trusted relationships is critically important in management. While you have the positional authority to drive your team forward, you may overlook the exponential opportunity that trusted relationships provide.

"Trust has depth. On the surface, one of your employees can trust that their co-worker will show up to work on time and work hard for most of the day. But deep trust provides insight to an individual's true self and motivations. Trust is one of those words that we seem to throw around a lot, filing off the raw edges of its true definition.

"Trust actually comes in different forms. There's predictive trust - which is knowing people will do what they say – and then there's vulnerability-based trust – which means people are open and honest with each other. As a leader, you probably see yourself as trustworthy, likely more trustworthy than those around you. But do others on your primary team see you that way? Do they **truly** trust you, and you them? Are you getting naked – so to speak – by becoming comfortable with letting your team and colleagues see you for who you really are?

"As the leader, it's your job to create an environment which enables employees to get to know each other, I mean really know each other, so that they can see others for who they really are with no pretension, no positioning."

"Okay, I understand you. Well at least intellectually," Jacob stated with a little bit of a grin. "Creating those types of relationships must take a lot of work but I can imagine the sweet payoff from the investment."

"The other area that feels strange for me recently is a feeling that I'm on unstable ground. Everything seems so new and I'm struggling with how inadequate I feel most days at work and at home."

"Well Jacob, to be honest when we struggle as leaders, we often feel inadequate. No matter what level you're at within an organization. We may wonder quietly why we took the job in the first place, but we definitely do not want to talk with others about our struggles, which is a shame.

"The struggles can create great strain though surprisingly this can be a good thing because times of great strain create defining moments in who we are and how we can lead. The struggle itself is the trigger that we can use to tell our reflective brains to listen up and learn something, especially after the fact while we are reflecting upon the events.

"There's a tension that all great struggles bring. The tension is a byproduct of change, and it forces leaders to be off-balance. While tension can come from various sources – tradition, relationships, aspirations, and identity – it's the automatic responses we develop to these tension points that can cause confusion. Self-exploration of these tension areas could provide insight as to *why* we are confused. And, by the way, telling others our stories could provide them with wisdom and insight as well.

"Unfortunately, leaders at all levels are fearful of telling their 'struggle stories' for fear of showing their weaknesses and failures. Ironically, it is in the telling of these stories that great insight can be found, not only for the storyteller but also for those listening.

"This cultural storytelling can be very useful for leaders. A good story can reveal so much about the culture of the team. The blending of experiences, people, events, successes, challenges, tragedies, and life converge within the team over time to create the existing culture.

"Great leaders work hard to build a culture they believe will allow the team to survive and excel over time. These leaders know that culture – good and bad – evolves over time and well-told stories reveal the threads of people and events that, when woven together, create desired aspects of the culture. Impactful leaders use the stories and history to paint the picture of the desired cultural state or cultural fabric.

"We have the same opportunity at home. Fathers in the current season of life where you are often overlook the value of the stories they can tell their kids to weave in the threads of the culture they want in their family. Stories of their earlier life – good and bad – provide the word pictures kids need to envision their dad in a similar life season.

"A really interesting success that we stumbled upon was the creation of 'parenting moments.' This is a term we derived to label the found time leaders experienced at home which were the outcome of 1) being more productive at work and 2) being happier when they left work. Once home, they were more apt to take advantage of these slivers of time with their kids and/or their spouse. These parenting moments, these slivers of time, come and go without any warning or replay. If you are there in the moment and fully engaged in that moment, you have the opportunity to fully leverage that time to notice a behavior, see an insight, answer or ask a question, and lock in with a small phrase, saying or story which captures the moment.

"Again and again we had leaders telling stories during their report-ins of their successes from the last week being little things at home which were really having an impact on the growth of their families and making them more engaged at work.

"While this seemed somewhat counterintuitive at first, when we really thought through how leaders become great, it is precisely because their whole life is trending well.

"So let's get to your homework. Over the next couple of weeks, I want you to work on improving every relationship you have at work and at home by one step forward. You'll need to make a list of every person that works for you and who is involved with you at home. Next to each person, write down the one small step you can take to slightly deepen the relationship.

"You're looking for very tiny steps here. Not enormous movements. An example at work might be that for a certain employee, you will take three minutes and ask about what frustrates them at work. An example for home might be you'll spend five minutes on the floor with your youngest kid looking at the world as they see it.

"The context of each tiny step isn't nearly as important as the energy you invest into the moment you choose. When we get together, I'll ask you to share your successes and stumbles with this homework."

CHUCK

Jacob found Chuck at the bar and ordered a beer. They caught up on families and life.

"So," Chuck asked "how did you make out at the conference? I've been curious what you thought of David and his story."

Jacob took a drink of his beer and hesitated a moment thinking about what to say to Chuck. "Well, he sure had my head hurting by the end of the day!"

They both laughed.

"I don't know Chuck; there was so much that happened that day and the following weeks as well. I ended up running into David – literally – in the hallway after his talk. He saved me from spilling everything on the floor as I juggled to hang on to my coffee while reaching to answer my phone."

"Is there video of the encounter?" Chuck said with a grin. "I'd love to see you awkwardly trying to juggle your coffee."

"Sure. It's gone viral. I'm getting more hits than that recent cat video." Jacob offered.

"I actually had a lot of time with David" Jacob continued. "I asked him a pointed question which led to a discussion which led to a longer discussion."

"David's awesome Jacob. If you got that much time with him, that's fantastic. What stuck with you from your time with David?'

"I'm basically a failure as a leader, as a father and as a husband," Jacob said almost too quickly. "I mean, I'm not a failure. It's that my eyes were opened to a new way of thinking. David had a great way of saying it. My glasses have been murky and after our conversation, the murkiness is starting to clear. I didn't know my glasses were murky but now that I do, it's really amazing."

Jacob went on to tell Chuck about what he'd been through since that day. He told him about the note, how he and Abby stayed up late talking the night he came home, about his *Everything DiSC®* assessments, and about his first 'reporting-in' session with David.

Chuck encouraged Jacob to stay on the path and get as much wisdom from David as possible. Chuck explained how David had had a tremendous impact on a peer of his at work. And how that peer had pulled Chuck into a series of group gatherings and shared the knowledge about leading well.

REPORT-IN #2

It was a cold, rainy day when Jacob and David met next. Jacob was excited to meet with David but also a bit apprehensive. He had worked hard on his "homework" but he felt like he had more stumbles than successes and wasn't sure how much to share with David.

"Hi Jacob!" David caught Jacob by surprise in that he was already set up at a table with coffee and lunch.

Jacob had arrived early, hoping to have a few minutes to gather his thoughts. But David had beat him there.

"So Jacob, tell me about the best meal you've had since we last met."

"I'm sorry, can you repeat that question?"

"Sure, what has been the best meal you've had since we last met?"

Jacob hesitated and stammered a bit before answering. "Well, I guess I'd say it was the client dinner a couple of weeks ago in Saratoga. We had what I think was the best steak I've ever had in my life."

"Sounds great Jacob," David said with a positive nod.

"So," David began. "Report in. Tell me what's been going on in your field of battle."

Jacob recounted several stories from the last couple of weeks and provided many examples of his successes and stumbles with employees and his family. One story in particular was hitting Jacob hard, which prompted David to dig a little deeper.

"Jacob, unpack that one a bit more for me. You said your tiny step forward with Jeff was to sit with him to watch how he processed a certain activity and your intention was to help Jeff learn how he was slowing down the process for the whole team. To train him up on how he could be more efficient and effective. Do I have that right?"

"Yep, that's exactly what I was looking for. But Jeff totally screwed up the process – again – and I had to take over his computer to show him how to fix the problem."

"Ok, I have tone." David said.

"What?"

"I've got tone."

"Oh yea, okay, you've got permission to fire."

"How do you think Jeff felt during the exchange and you taking over his computer? What did he learn? What's the story in his head?"

"Wow! He's probably not very happy." Jacob said strongly. "And given his communications style, he's likely never going to show how uncomfortable he was. Man I blew that one."

"It's okay Jacob." David offered in a warm, consoling tone. "You're working on adjusting habits to create a new trend line and the stumbles with those habit changes offer the best stories you can tell.

"It sounds a bit like you are trying to go too quickly with Jeff. Think of your mix of engagement as a gas pedal with one extreme being too little direction – not enough gas – and the other extreme being the 'move out of the way and let me show you how it's done', which has the pedal to the floor. Great leaders who lead well have learned how to adjust the gas pedal smoothly in a split second just as you would in a car. You're new at this, and currently trying to use your left foot on the gas pedal. The smoothness of change isn't quite there yet.

"Tell me about your home life; what's been going on there?"

Jacob ran through his list of successes and stumbles, recounting how he figured out that his expectations of his kids were way out-of-whack for their personal styles. He had always thought he should be exactly the same with each kid but now realizes how different his kids are from one another and how he must adjust his interactions in order to be a better father.

Jacob and Abby's relationship was improving. He told David about the couple of date nights they had enjoyed and his slowly evolving insight to when Abby's style and his meshed well and when they didn't. He had found several opportunities to thank Abby for what he would previously had thought to be very minor things, but now realized how important those little "thank yous" were to Abby.

David praised Jacob for his effort in providing more substance during his report-in and the insight he was beginning to gain at work and at home.

"Jacob, let's close out our time here and let me give you a little homework. Over the next month I want you to look at your team at work and your team at home with a new lens. Once a day you need to replay the movie of your team. Take on the role of the producer for a reality TV show. You have all this video footage of the team in action during the day and you also have access to those private moments when each employee would describe how they're really feeling about others on the team.

"The first couple of days you try this exercise, you will likely be a bit overwhelmed with the vast amount of information flooding into your brain. After a few days of practice, you'll be able to move through the video at a faster rate, recognizing when you need to slow down the replay in order to really catch an interaction. At least that's the experience many of our leaders had as they went through the process.

"I want you to also do the video replay exercise with your family time. What are the interactions, the conversations that are occurring? How are your kids reacting and how does Abby engage with you? Be very selective regarding the time of day and location you decide to use for 'viewing' the replay. You will need to make sure you are devoting your full brain to the reviews."

REPORT-IN #3

Jacob and David met at the same Panera Bread but this time Jacob was there ahead of David. He invested the time to review his notes on what was important for his report-in

"Good morning Jacob, thanks for grabbing us a spot to meet."

"No worries. I've been here for a while and found the time relaxing."

"Great," said David. "So, Jacob tell me about the best meal you've had since we last met."

There was that crazy question again, Jacob thought. Why on earth does he care about the best meal I've had?

Jacob thought for a moment and told David about a lunch he was invited to at a new restaurant in town that fully lived up to its reviews. As he told the story of the meal he kept feeling like he was missing something.

David followed up "sounds like a fine meal Jacob. So, that was the best meal you had? Huh."

David and Jacob then caught up on Jacob's video review exercises. Jacob talked in depth about what he saw in this virtual world of his employees and their likely conversations and how they probably really felt about interactions. And David had been right, the first couple days were really hard and confusing. But as time went on he was able to fast forward through a lot of video then slowing down for specific segments.

Jacob recounted how he could almost anticipate how some of his employees were going to react to his behavior as he saw the video playing out. And he was super surprised to see the intra-team connections which he realized he so often overlooked.

Next Jacob described the difficulty he had in performing the video review for his home life. The cadence of life at home was not as consistent over the week as it was at work. So performing the review for a Saturday was much more difficult than a Tuesday when he only saw his family for a short period of time. Also, he found it hard to isolate time to make sure he was thinking just about family. He had tried at first to use his commute time into work as his video replay window but quickly found he was merging thoughts of work for the upcoming day with the family video.

Ultimately, he found the best time to perform the review was as he settled down after the kids had gone to bed. Instead of pulling out his laptop to catchup on emails and other work items, he simply sank into his favorite chair and stared off at a family picture across the room.

Jacob then asked "David, why is it so simple to slide work thoughts into time at home but not the other way around? And why when I'm going through the video exercise do I always start with my kids and leave Abby for last? And why does that time I spend reviewing the family videos fly by and take so much longer than my work videos?

"And why do I fast forward some of the work video but hardly ever fast forward my family video? And in fact there were some times I actually slowed down the family video to slow motion. Why is that?"

David smiled at Jacob and let the questions hang in the air. David recognized this moment for exactly what it was: Jacob had just crossed the threshold into a perspective of his world from which he would likely never return. His capacity to see the full tension between home and work and the inequality that he had allowed between the two. And just how important his family and life at home was to him.

David answered the question with a question, "Of the two sets of video reviews – work and home – which had you smiling more?"

A smile poured across Jacob's face as the answer came clearly into focus. "Hands down, my family videos."

"You're doing great Jacob! Now let's talk about your homework. Over the next month I want you to read the book *The Five Dysfunctions of a Team* and be prepared to talk about the team model that Patrick Lencioni reveals in his book and how you gauge the cohesiveness of your team at work and how functional you gauge your family to be. Got it?"

"Yup, I'm with you. Just thinking about those videos. Wow, I didn't see that coming."

THE FINAL REPORT-IN

Jacob and David arrived together, parking within two spaces of each other in the parking lot of the Panera Bread. They exchanged small talk as they went inside, ordered and found a table next to the fireplace.

"So Jacob, tell me about the best meal you've had since we last met."

Jacob thought, damn, there's that same question again. He began thinking through the various meals he had had since they last met 5 weeks ago. There was a great client dinner that solidified a contract for his company which was extremely important. Then there was the anniversary dinner he and Abby had gone on which was tremendous. "David, the best meal I've had since we last met was my anniversary dinner with Abby which was fantastic."

"Okay, that's good to hear Jacob."

Jacob was underwhelmed with David's response. There must be something he's missing. *What is it?* he thought.

David interrupted Jacob's thoughts "So, Jacob, report in, tell me what's been going on. How did you progress with your homework assignment?"

Jacob started with a recap of the book; his takeaways regarding the simplicity of the team model and how he saw some of the characters from the book on his team as well as among his peers. He showed David the graphic he'd drawn up, illustrating the model and a crossover to corresponding cohesive team behavior concepts. He had found the graphic on the website of a firm which had been delivering some team development services with the executive team at work.

Jacob told David how the conversation they had had early on regarding the true definition of trust came through so clearly in the team model. He was very excited about the opportunity for healthy conflict within his team but concerned that his team needed help to navigate to a healthy place where they truly trusted each other so that they could have the opportunity for healthy conflict.

David listened patiently, encouraging Jacob in his deep thinking on team dynamics and his rating of where he felt his work team landed.

"So" David prompted Jacob "tell me about how you viewed the functionality of your family in relation to the team model that Patrick Lencioni wrote about.

"Well," Jacob began "the model can fully lay over top of my family model. The main difference I noticed is the implicit authority that is evident in my and Abby's roles in our family and the difficulty that could create in allowing for open, healthy conflict. Our kids are not equipped to discuss and debate some family decisions as such non-equals. But when Abby and I talked this through. . ."

"Hold on" David interrupted "you and Abby discussed the book? Has she read the book?"

"Heck yea." Jacob enthusiastically stated. "She picked the book up one evening while I was having some fun wrestling with the kids. She stayed up into the early morning to finish it because she said she just couldn't put it down.

"We spent the next couple of nights talking about the model, our current family, and probably more importantly, how the dysfunction within the families we grew up in created such obstacles to our perceptions of how we each viewed a functional family. We had some great conversations and created a hand-written agreement outlining how we wanted to facilitate enabling trust and engaging conversations with our kids to help them learn how to have healthy conflict as they grow."

Suddenly a video started replaying in Jacob's head. There he was, sitting with his kids and Abby at the table having a meal together and while he couldn't recall the food they had had, he could clearly see his kids giggling at the story he was telling of a time when he was a kid. And then he sees Abby, smiling a warm, loving smile that only a wife truly in love with her husband as a man and as an engaged father to her kids can hold.

"David," Jacob said somewhat loudly "I want to change my answer to a question you asked earlier. The best meal I've had since we last met was a simple meal with my family about two weeks ago. I have no idea what we ate or even exactly which day it was, but it was truly the best meal I've had in a very, very long time."

David smiled at Jacob and said assuredly "Now THAT is a best meal."

After a seemingly awkward pause that both men allowed to last as long as needed, they began talking about Jacob's growth since they first met and Jacob's dreams for his next season of life at work and with his family.

GOING THE DISTANCE

As Jacob and David stood in the parking lot ready to leave, Jacob broke the silence "So David, what's next for me? What's my homework?"

David responded, "Well Jacob, the best course of action for you now is to pay it forward. To make what you've learned stick, you need to find a peer and coach them up on all that you've learned.

"It's way too easy to take some gained wisdom and let it slowly slip into history and then before we know it, we're behaving in our old ways. Connecting deeply with a peer manager will force you to be wise in leading them forward with the knowledge of leading well. And the act of teaching or coaching will cement your learning into habits.

"And we know from our experiences that it's always better for two to be in it together. A friend of mine told me once of a conversation he had with the Chief of the Navy Seals. My friend asked the Chief why there are always pairs of Seals being deployed. The Chief explained that if you send two men into battle the fear factor is cut tremendously because each man will focus on taking care of the buddy. They draw courage from each other, they drive each other and they achieve a tremendous amount more than two men working separately. They are in it together and propel each other further.

"One of the main factors in our achieving success in building the leadership capacity of our area was the multiplier effect of leaders drawing each other forward because they were in it together. We purposely pulled small groups of leaders – three to five at a time – together for small group coaching sessions. In the beginning we basically forced them to talk with each other, sharing their stories from the field of leadership. After a few such gatherings, the leaders started really opening up about what was working – their successes – and where they had some missteps – their stumbles.

"It sounds so simple as I say it to you. And in reality, it is really that simple. Leaders need to be with other leaders and be discussing their trade so that they pass along wisdom.

"So that's what I think you should do. Grab a peer and make them meet with you. Model the behaviors of leading well. Reveal your stumbles and be vulnerable. Once you have one on board, grab another to join in. And then another. When the small group seems too big, spin off and start another while still checking in on the first group."

Jacob looked off into the field next to the parking lot and thought about David's challenge. "You know David; I think I really get it. If I treat my peers just as I do my employees, earning the right to lead them as a peer, then they will 'taste' the magic."

"That's exactly right Jacob."

David and Jacob started to shake hands and then David pulled Jacob in for a manly hug.

As Jacob drove down the highway towards home, he thought deeply about the journey he'd been on. He was excited to grab one of his peers and share the knowledge he gained. But he also was a bit nervous. Would they really accept him in that role? He realized he had no choice but to lead forward. He couldn't, wouldn't go back to his old habits and wanted desperately to keep his employees and family trending forward fully engaged.

ABOUT THE AUTHOR

Michael Holland unravels the mysteries of leadership. Michael is a professional executive coach and trusted advisor to executives who seek to become better leaders and build cohesive teams. Michael's wisdom and insight are the product of 30 plus years of leadership experience and an uncanny, natural ability to perceive the questions that need to be asked.

Michael founded Bishop House Consulting in 1999 to provide organizational leadership expertise and team development services to companies experiencing dynamic change. Michael has provided distinguished executive coaching services to well over 400 leaders in organizations ranging from start-ups to multi-billion dollar corporations. Michael earned his MBA from the University of

Baltimore and is the author of **_Leadership Learning Moments_**, a weekly inspiration – or reminder – regarding the critical role leaders play in the lives of employees.

In addition to his role as President of Bishop House Consulting, Michael currently serves on the Area Committee for Young Life Capital Region, invests his time and energy instigating men who seek more purpose in life, is a believing Christian, and is active in the Burnt Hills, NY community where he and his wife raised and launched three children into the world.

You can connect with Michael here:

LinkedIn: mikeatbishophouse
Twitter: @mikehollandatbh
Email: mike@bishophouse.com
Personal Blog: www.instigatingmen.com

You can learn more about Michael's firm, Bishop House Consulting, here:

www.bishophouse.com

Notes

Notes

Notes

Notes

49804078R00059

Made in the USA
San Bernardino, CA
05 June 2017